This Book Belongs To

____

Easy Planners And Journals
To help you organize your life

This book is copyright protected. Reproducing this book is prohibited and not allowed without the permission of the author. All rights reserved.

www.ingramcontent.com/pod-product-compliance
Lightning Source LLC
Chambersburg PA
CBHW071219240726
48654CB00009B/846